Collins

easy lea

Maths

puzzles

Ages 8-9

Peter Clarke

About this book

This book will help your child consolidate their mathematical understanding and develop problem-solving skills, logical thinking and mathematical reasoning.

Puzzles can help your child:

- enjoy and engage with mathematics by seeing a purpose in what they are doing
- develop their ability to identify patterns and make connections
- use and apply their existing mathematical knowledge
- work systematically
- make and test deductions and generalisations, account for all possibilities and establish a proof
- develop their working memory
- develop their ability to cope with challenging situations and to persevere.

All the above will benefit your child in other areas of learning and real life too!

How to use this book

- Find a quiet, comfortable place to work, away from distractions.
- Tackle one puzzle at a time. The puzzles are not in a particular order, so your child can choose any puzzle that interests them.
- Help with reading the instructions where necessary and ensure that your child understands what they are required to do.
- Give your child a pencil and eraser so they can easily change an answer if they need to.
- If your child is struggling to complete a puzzle, encourage them to persevere.
  If necessary, refer to the solution and fill in one or two of the missing numbers or answers to give them some help. Let them take a break and return to it at another time.
- Help and encourage your child to check their own answers as they complete each puzzle.
- Reward your child with plenty of praise and encouragement.

Special features

 This symbol indicates the mathematics that your child needs to know and the concepts that they are practising while working on the puzzle.

 Ask your child to colour a star to show how easy or hard they found each puzzle.

Published by Collins
An imprint of HarperCollins*Publishers*
1 London Bridge Street
London SE1 9GF

Browse the complete Collins catalogue at
www.collins.co.uk

© HarperCollins*Publishers* Limited 2018

10 9 8 7 6 5 4 3 2 1

ISBN 978-0-00-826605-9

The author asserts the moral right to be identified as the author of this work.

British Library Cataloguing in Publication Data
A Catalogue record for this publication is available from the British Library

The author wishes to thank Brian Molyneaux for his valuable contribution to this publication.

Author: Peter Clarke
Commissioning Editor: Michelle I'Anson
Editor and Project Manager: Rebecca Skinner
Cover design by Sarah Duxbury
Inside concept Design by Paul Oates
Page layout by Q2A Media Services PVT Ltd.
Illustration: Jenny Tulip
Production: Lyndsey Rogers
Printed and bound in China by RR Donnelley APS

Number search

Find each number below hidden in the grid and draw a ring around it.

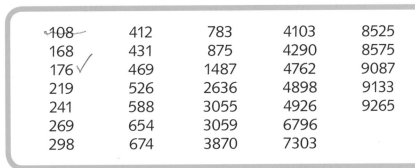

Horizontally means across (left to right). Vertically means from top to bottom. Diagonally means in a sloping direction.

The numbers can run horizontally, vertically and diagonally.

The numbers can only run forwards (not backwards).

Each digit in the grid can only be used once.

108	412	783	4103	8525
168	431	875	4290	8575
176	469	1487	4762	9087
219	526	2636	4898	9133
241	588	3055	4926	9265
269	654	3059	6796	
298	674	3870	7303	

9	2	4	9	2	6	2	1	5	7	8	3
1	3	0	5	9	1	0	3	8	2	7	6
3	7	2	6	1	0	4	1	8	9	3	7
3	0	1	2	5	8	1	3	7	8	0	9
4	3	9	3	5	4	0	8	1	6	3	6
1	7	0	4	3	1	3	7	2	2	6	9
2	4	3	5	4	8	4	0	9	4	7	8
4	2	9	0	5	8	5	4	5	6	1	7
9	1	5	0	6	2	9	7	6	4	9	5
6	7	4	2	0	6	5	8	5	9	2	1
8	5	2	5	6	3	9	0	8	7	6	6
1	4	8	7	0	6	4	7	6	2	5	8

 Read numbers with up to four digits in numerals.

Just right

Easy   Hard

How did you find it?

1 to 9 totals

A column is a vertical block of squares (from top to bottom). A row is a horizontal block of squares (from left to right).

Fill in the blank squares using the digits 1 to 9.

Use each digit only once in each grid.

The sum of the three digits in each column, row and diagonal must equal the number in the orange box.

Grid 1

			15
	2		15
			9
	8		21
16	15	14	21

Grid 2

			16
		1	10
			16
	3		19
16	13	16	18

Easy **Just right** Hard

How did you find it?

Add three one-digit numbers.

Arrange 1 to 9

Fill in the empty squares using the digits 1 to 9.

0, 1, 2, 3, 4, 5, 6, 7, 8 and 9 are digits. They are used to write numbers, e.g. the number 15 is made up of two digits: 1 and 5.

Use each digit only once in each grid.

The sum of the four squares around each circle must be equal to the number in the circle.

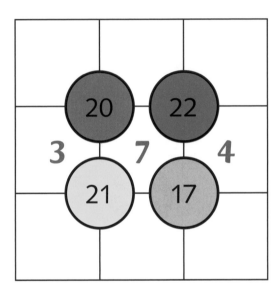

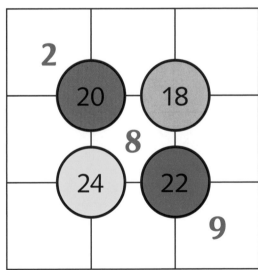

 Add four one-digit numbers.

How did you find it?

Linking shapes

Draw horizontal and vertical lines through the squares to connect matching shapes.

Every square on the grid must have one line passing through it.

Lines cannot cross and no diagonal lines are allowed.

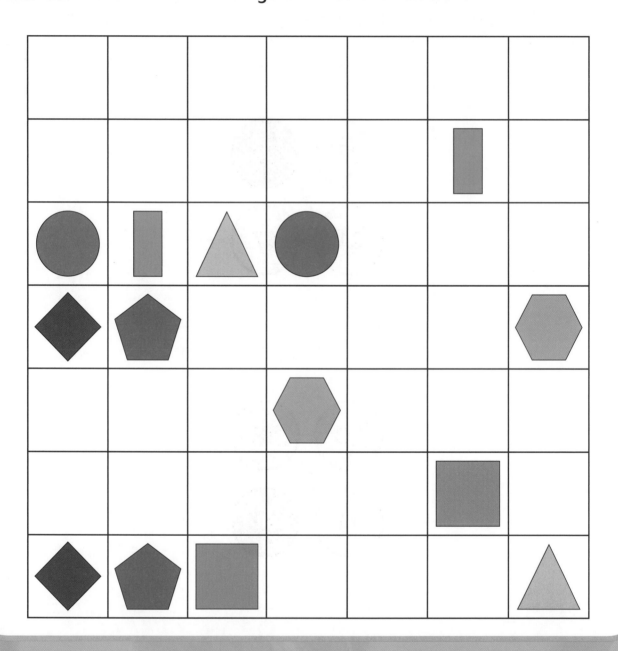

How did you find it?

Identify horizontal and vertical lines.
Use reasoning and logical thinking skills.

Kakuro

Write a digit from 1 to 9 in each empty square so that:

- the sum of each horizontal block equals the number in the triangle on its left
- the sum of each vertical block equals the number in the triangle at the top.

No digit can be used more than once in the same block.

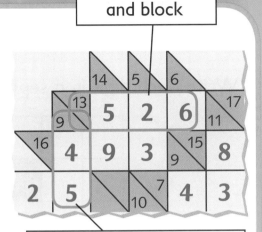

Horizontal clue and block

Vertical clue and block

Add two or more numbers mentally.
Identify and use patterns and relationships involving numbers.

Just right
Easy
Hard
How did you find it?

Fill in the digits

Write each of the numbers below onto the grid.

Write each digit in a separate square.

			■			■			
		■	5	3	8	9	■		
		3	■			■	4	9	8
■		9			■				■
	■	5		■	7			■	
		9	■		4			■	
■		■			5	■			
4	9	1	8	■	7		■		■
			■	3	■				■
	■			1		■			

20	64	208	654	1692	~~5389~~
29	65	268	691	2580	5673
~~31~~	67	402	719	3298	6351
32	73	475	725	3518	6485
48	96	476	728	~~3959~~	~~7457~~
51	97	~~498~~	763	3961	
52	153	532	768	4235	
61	173	582	939	~~4918~~	

How did you find it?

 Recognise place value in numbers with up to four digits.

Cross maths

For each puzzle, write the four numbers from the circles in the grid.

The two rows and two columns must make four correct calculations.

All calculations must be performed in order, from left to right and top to bottom.

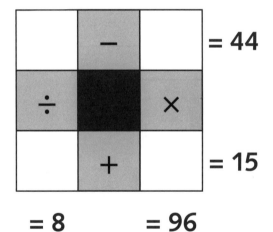

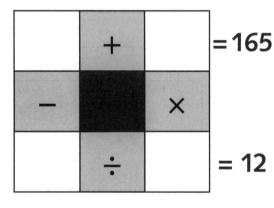

Divide and share

Draw three straight lines across each rectangle from edge to edge.

Position your lines so that each rectangle is divided into six sections.

Each section must contain two different fish.

Easy   Just right   Hard

How did you find it?

Identify and use patterns and relationships involving geometry.

Cross maths 1 to 9

Write the digits 1 to 9 in the white squares.

The three rows and three columns must make six correct calculations.

All calculations must be performed in order, from left to right and top to bottom.

	×		+		= 51
×		×		×	
	×		÷		= 4
+		÷		−	
	×	4	+		= 17

= 10　　　　　= 12　　　　　= 13

Add and subtract numbers mentally.
Recall multiplication and division facts for the multiplication tables up to 12 × 12.

How did you find it?
Easy　Just right　Hard

11

Re-value

Rearrange all the digits in each of the black boxes and write one digit in each of the white boxes to the right ➤ and / or below ▼.

Column clues (▼): 512, 3652, 5718, 72, 124, 172, 9604

Row/other clues:
- 6122 ➤, 742 ➤, 1356 ▼
- 8275 ➤, 2061 ➤
- 531 ➤, 345 ▼, 9145 ➤
- 4725 ➤▼, 8917 ▼, 16 ➤
- 6981 ▼, 4596 ➤▼, **5 6 9 4**, 2057 ▼
- 1536 ➤, **6**, 741 ➤, 813 ▼
- 994 ➤, **9**, 83 ➤▼, 35 ➤▼
- 8537 ➤, **5**, 2751 ➤
- 4628 ➤, **4**, 803 ➤

Recognise place value in numbers with up to four digits.

Brain teasers

Start with the number on the left.

Follow the instructions from left to right.

Write your final answer in the empty box.

15 → + 6 → × 2 → ÷ 7 → + 38 → − 8 → $\frac{2}{3}$ of it → ☐

8 → × 12 → + 4 → ÷ 10 → + 2 → $\frac{3}{4}$ of it → × 8 → ☐

63 → ÷ 9 → + 57 → $\frac{1}{8}$ of it → × 6 → − 30 → ÷ 6 → ☐

72 → − 9 → ÷ 7 → + 3 → × 8 → − 60 → $\frac{5}{6}$ of it → ☐

45 → $\frac{5}{9}$ of it → − 9 → ÷ 4 → + 8 → × 3 → $\frac{1}{6}$ of it → ☐

 Add and subtract numbers mentally.
Recall multiplication and division facts for the
multiplication tables up to 12 × 12.
Find fractions of numbers.

Easy Just right Hard

How did you find it?

Follow the arrows

Start in the top left-hand corner.

Follow the arrows around the map, e.g.
3 ← means 'move three places to the left'.

Eventually you will land on an object.

Circle that object.

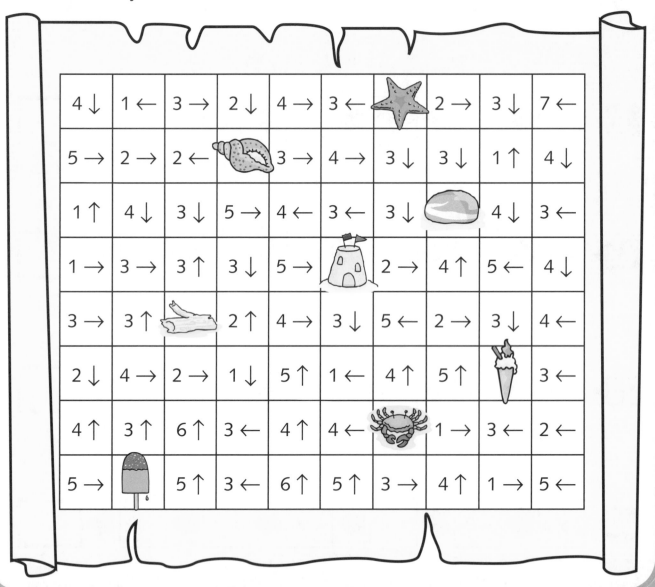

4 ↓	1 ←	3 →	2 ↓	4 →	3 ←	⭐	2 →	3 ↓	7 ←
5 →	2 →	2 ←	🐚	3 →	4 →	3 ↓	3 ↓	1 ↑	4 ↓
1 ↑	4 ↓	3 ↓	5 →	4 ←	3 ←	3 ↓	🪨	4 ↓	3 ←
1 →	3 →	3 ↑	3 ↓	5 →	🏰	2 →	4 ↑	5 ←	4 ↓
3 →	3 ↑	🪵	2 ↑	4 →	3 ↓	5 ←	2 →	3 ↓	4 ←
2 ↓	4 →	2 →	1 ↓	5 ↑	1 ←	4 ↑	5 ↑	🍦	3 ←
4 ↑	3 ↑	6 ↑	3 ←	4 ↑	4 ←	🦀	1 →	3 ←	2 ←
5 →		5 ↑	3 ←	6 ↑	5 ↑	3 →	4 ↑	1 →	5 ←

Follow instructions involving position, direction and movement.

14

Sum-times

Each number in the grid is made by adding or multiplying a pair of numbers from the circles.

Each pair of numbers should be used twice:

- once as an addition
- once as a multiplication.

Write each calculation below its answer.

One has already been done for you.

132	36	30	49
		10 × 3	
7	360	420	24
180	23	58	10
13	400	67	80
10 + 3			

② ~~③~~ ④ ⑤ ⑥ ⑦ ⑧ ⑨ ~~⑩~~ ⑪ ⑫ ⑳ ㉚ ㊵ ㊿ 60

 Add numbers mentally.
Recall and use multiplication facts for the multiplication tables up to 12 × 12.

How did you find it?

Futoshiki

Write a digit from 1 to 5 in each empty box.

Follow the greater than (>) and less than (<) signs to compare single-digit numbers in adjacent boxes.

You can only use each digit once in each column and row.

Adjacent boxes are next to each other.

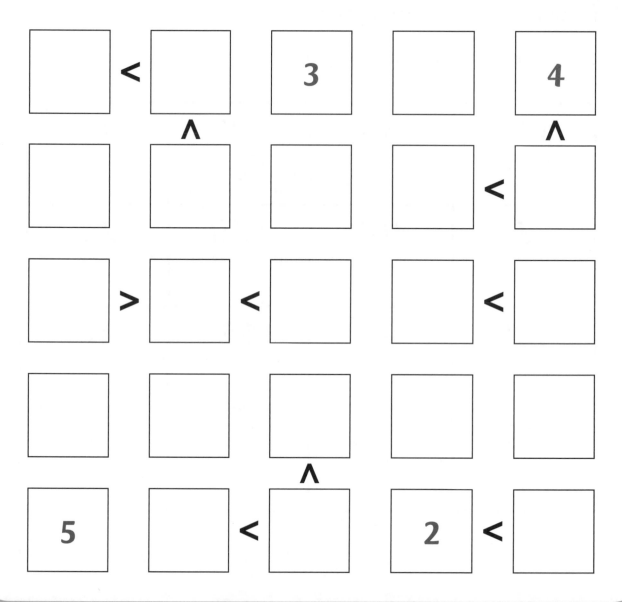

Compare and order numbers using the < and > signs.

Just right
Easy
Hard

How did you find it?

16

Difference–divisions

Each number in the grid is made by subtracting or dividing a pair of numbers from the circles.

Each pair of numbers should be used twice:
- once as a subtraction
- once as a division.

Write each calculation below its answer.

One has already been done for you.

8	24	40	6
			36 ÷ 6
18	9	4	48
5	49	11	80
30	7	10	3
36 − 6			

(3) (4) (5) (~~6~~) (7) (8) (10) (12) (15) (21) (32) (~~36~~) (44) (56) (60) (90)

 Subtract numbers mentally.
Recall division facts for the multiplication tables up to 12 × 12.

Easy   Just right   Hard

How did you find it?

Find the treasure

Start in the top left-hand corner.

Follow the directions around the map, e.g. 3 W means 'move three places to the west'.

Eventually you will land on an item of treasure.

Circle that item.

The points of a compass are north, south, east and west. Check these directions on the diagram above the map if you need to.

3 S	1 S	2 E	4 S	3 E	4 E	3 W	2 S		6 S
4 E	4 S		3 S	3 W	2 E	5 W	1 W	5 W	2 S
3 S	2 E	1 W	5 S		4 S	2 N	4 W	3 W	1 W
4 E	2 N	2 S	2 N	2 S	4 E		1 N	6 W	2 N
1 S		2 W	3 E	3 N	3 S	2 S	2 S	2 S	4 W
5 W	6 E	5 N	3 W	2 S	2 E	1 S	1 E	3 N	
3 E	4 N	1 S	5 E	4 E	6 N	6 W		3 N	2 N
	7 E	4 N	3 W	3 W	2 E	6 N	3 N	6 N	5 W

How did you find it?

Easy · Just right · Hard

Follow instructions involving position, direction and movement.

18

KenKen

Operators are the symbols that tell you to add (+), subtract (−), multiply (×) or divide (÷).

Write a digit from 1 to 4 in each square in the grid.

Each digit can be used only once in each row and column.

A target number and operator is given for each block with a bold black outline.

For example, 10 + means the target number is 10 and the operator is +, so the digits in that block must add up to 10.

4 +		9 +	
24 ×			1 −
	4 ×		
	8+		

2 ÷	2 −	3 ×	6 +
8 +	8 ×		
		5 +	

 Add, subtract, multiply and divide numbers mentally.
Multiply together three numbers.

Ordering

Write a number from 1 to 49 in each square.

You can only use each number once.

The numbers must run in order, starting from 1, to form a path.

The path can travel horizontally or vertically, but not diagonally. For example, 2 must be alongside, above or below 1.

47			42			37
		44		40		
			6			
12		8		4		32
			2			
		20		24		
17			22			29

Easy   Just right   Hard

How did you find it?

Order numbers from 1 to 49.

Missing operators

For each calculation, write a different operator in each circle: +, −, × or ÷.

9 $\bigcirc$ 3 $\left(+\right)$ 7 $\bigcirc$ 5 = 5

6 $\left(\times\right)$ 8 $\bigcirc$ 9 $\bigcirc$ 3 = 42

12 $\bigcirc$ 4 $\left(-\right)$ 2 $\bigcirc$ 6 = 7

7 $\bigcirc$ 9 $\bigcirc$ 5 $\left(-\right)$ 8 = 60

8 $\left(\div\right)$ 2 $\bigcirc$ 9 $\bigcirc$ 1 = 35

 Add and subtract numbers mentally.
Recall and use multiplication and division facts for the multiplication tables up to 12 × 12.

Moving to X

Move through the 25 circles following the instructions on each circle.

For example, 2D means to move two places down.

Work out where to start (1), so that you finish on the circle marked with an **X** (25).

Number the circles 1 to 24, stopping on each circle just once.

4D	1R	4D	2L	4L
1D	1R	2D	3D	2D
2R	3R	1R	1U	2U
3R	1U	1L	3U	4L
X 25	3U	1L	1R	3U

Easy   Just right   Hard

How did you find it?

Follow instructions involving position, direction and movement.

Symbols

Each symbol stands for a digit from 1 to 7.

The number at the end of each row and column is the sum of the digits in it.

Work out which digit each of the five symbols stands for.

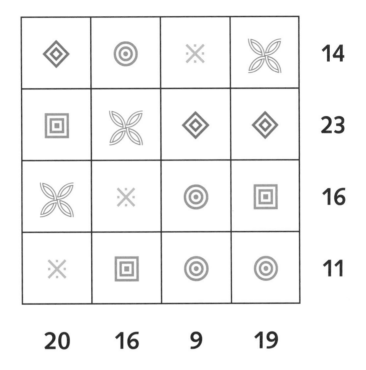

Record the digit that each symbol stands for in the table below.

✿	◈	◎	✳	▣
	5			

Add four one-digit numbers.

How did you find it?

Multiples madness

Shade three digits in each column and row.

The sum of the three shaded digits must be a multiple of the number in the circle.

	⑥	③	⑧	④
⑦	6	1	3	5
⑨	3	8	7	2
②	9	5	1	4
⑤	1	2	6	7

 Recognise multiples of 2, 3, 4, 5, 6, 7, 8 and 9.

24

Alphabet numerals

Replace each letter with a digit from 1 to 9.

Identical letters must be replaced by the same digit.

Each digit can only be used for one letter.

```
    F  B  G  D
 +  I  D  B  F
 ─────────────
    C  A  A  E
```

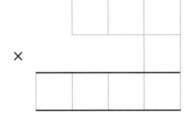

```
    A  G  B  H
 -  E  C  D  I
 ─────────────
    D  G  A  D
```

```
       E  F  C
 ×           A
 ─────────────
    E  E  H  I
```

Record the digit that each letter stands for in the table below.

A	B	C	D	E	F	G	H	I
7				1	6			

 Use written methods to add, subtract and multiply numbers.

Coloured balloons

Use the clues to colour the balloons and solve the puzzle.

There is only one correct solution.

1. There are 3 red (R) balloons, 3 blue (B) balloons, 3 green (G) balloons and 1 yellow (Y) balloon.

2. Both rows have a red (R) balloon, a blue (B) balloon and a green (G) balloon, appearing in that order from left to right.

3. All three green (G) balloons are either directly above or below a red (R) balloon.

4. Two blue (B) balloons are directly to the right of red (R) balloons.

5. The other blue (B) balloon is directly to the left of a red (R) balloon.

6. The yellow (Y) balloon is on the top row in the right-hand half of the puzzle.

Easy   Just right   Hard

How did you find it?

Follow instructions involving position, direction and movement.
Use reasoning and logical thinking skills.

Cross-number puzzle

This is like a crossword puzzle, but all the answers are numbers.

Write one digit in each square.

Across

1   Round 467 to the nearest 10
3   Days in 6 weeks
4   5700 ÷ 100
6   8462 − 3784
8   174 ÷ 6
9   Value of Roman numeral LXXXVI
10 6 × 7 × 8
11 Round 34·7 to the nearest whole number
14 84 × 7
17 6·8 m in cm
19 1000 more than 27
23 62 cm in mm
24 Area of a square with sides 6 cm

Down

1   58 × 7
2   4275 + 3468
5   253 + 187 + 266
7   289 × 8
12 12·83 + 18·17
13 Minutes in 6 hours
15 8·6 × 10
16 687 × 6
18 6 + 200 + 8000 + 50
19 $\frac{1}{9} \times 108$
20 208 ÷ 8
21 Months in 4 years
22 $\frac{5}{6} \times 42$

 Recall and use knowledge involving numbers, addition, subtraction, multiplication, division, fractions and decimals. Convert between different units of measure.

Easy   Just right   Hard

How did you find it?

Logic puzzle

One Saturday morning, Nasreen, David, Amir, Josie and Afia went to a car boot sale.

Each person bought one item. The items bought were a book, an electronic game, a dress, a DVD and a board game.

The prices paid were £1.50, £3, £4.50, £6 and £12.

Using the clues and the table below, work out:
- the item that each person bought
- how much they spent on their item.

1. David spent the most money. Josie spent more than Afia who didn't spend the least.

2. Amir and David both bought games. Afia didn't buy the dress.

3. Nasreen loves clothes and was very happy with her item. Josie bought something to read.

4. The board game was the least expensive item.

5. Nasreen spent a whole number of pounds. Afia spent exactly half as much as Nasreen.

Person	Item	Price
David		£12

Easy Just right Hard

How did you find it?

Use reasoning and logical thinking skills.

Solutions

Page 3: Number search

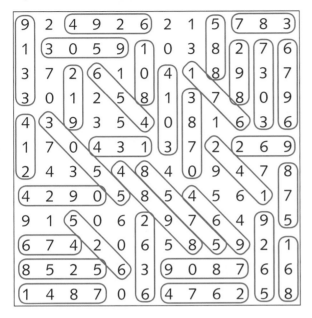

Page 4: 1 to 9 totals

			15
9	2	4	15
1	5	3	9
6	8	7	21
16	15	14	21

			16
5	4	1	10
2	6	8	16
9	3	7	19
16	13	16	18

Page 5: Arrange 1 to 9

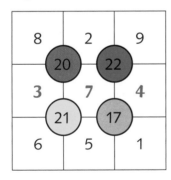

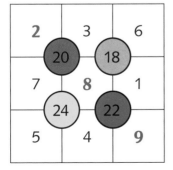

Page 6: Linking shapes

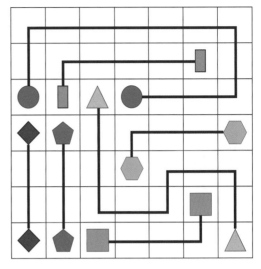

Page 7: Kakuro

	13	12	13		6	18	14
18	6	3	9	10	1	4	5
10	5	1	4	11 / 5	3	6	2
10	2	8	18 / 8	1	2	8	7
	10	17	7 / 3	4	14	15	14
14	2	7	5	9 / 6	1	3	2
9	3	6	28	8	9	4	7
9	5	4	18	1	4	8	5

Page 8: Fill in the digits

6	5	4		6	5		5	3	2
9	6		5	3	8	9		2	0
1	7	3		5	2		4	9	8
	3	9	6	1		7	2	8	
9		5	1		7	6	3		9
7	1	9		6	4	8	5		3
	6		4	7	5			2	9
4	9	1	8		7	3		5	
7	2	5		3		2	6	8	
6		3	5	1	8		4	0	2

Page 9: Cross maths

56	−	12	= 44
÷	■	×	
7	+	8	= 15
= 8		= 96	

144	+	21	= 165
−	■	×	
108	÷	9	= 12
= 36		= 189	

Page 10: Divide and share

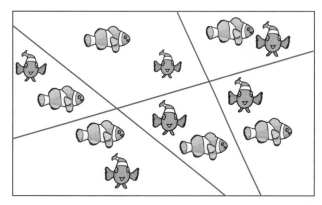

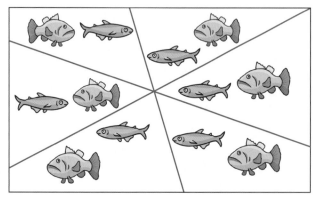

7	×	6	+	9	= 51
×	■	×	■	×	
1	×	8	÷	2	= 4
+	■	÷	■	−	
3	×	4	+	5	= 17
= 10		= 12		= 13	

Page 12: Re-value

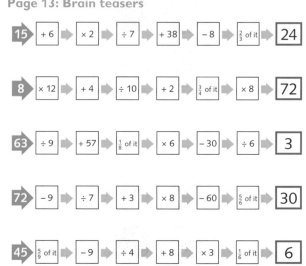

Page 13: Brain teasers

15 → + 6 → × 2 → ÷ 7 → + 38 → − 8 → $\frac{2}{3}$ of it → **24**

8 → × 12 → + 4 → ÷ 10 → + 2 → $\frac{3}{4}$ of it → × 8 → **72**

63 → ÷ 9 → + 57 → $\frac{1}{8}$ of it → × 6 → − 30 → ÷ 6 → **3**

72 → − 9 → ÷ 7 → + 3 → × 8 → − 60 → $\frac{5}{6}$ of it → **30**

45 → $\frac{5}{9}$ of it → − 9 → ÷ 4 → + 8 → × 3 → $\frac{1}{6}$ of it → **6**

132	36	30	49
11 × 12	30 + 6	10 × 3	40 + 9
7	**360**	**420**	**24**
2 + 5	40 × 9	60 × 7	20 + 4
180	**23**	**58**	**10**
30 × 6	11 + 12	50 + 8	2 × 5
13	**400**	**67**	**80**
10 + 3	50 × 8	60 + 7	20 × 4

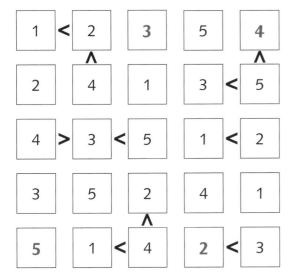

1 <	2	3	5	4
	∧			∧
2	4	1	3 <	5
4 >	3 <	5	1 <	2
3	5	2	4	1
		∧		
5	1 <	4	2 <	3

8	24	40	6
56 ÷ 7	32 − 8	44 − 4	36 ÷ 6
18	**9**	**4**	**48**
21 − 3	90 ÷ 10	32 ÷ 8	60 − 12
5	**49**	**11**	**80**
60 ÷ 12	56 − 7	44 ÷ 4	90 − 10
30	**7**	**10**	**3**
36 − 6	21 ÷ 3	15 − 5	15 ÷ 5

4 + 1	3	9 + 2	4
24 × 4	2	1	1 − 3
3	4 × 1	4	2
2	8 + 4	3	1

2 ÷ 4	2 − 3	3 × 1	6 + 2
2	1	3	4
8 + 3	8 × 2	4	1
1	4	5 + 2	3

31

Page 20: Ordering

47	46	45	**42**	41	38	**37**
48	49	**44**	43	**40**	39	36
11	10	7	**6**	5	34	35
12	9	**8**	3	**4**	33	**32**
13	14	1	**2**	25	26	31
16	15	**20**	21	**24**	27	30
17	18	19	**22**	23	28	**29**

Page 21: Missing operators

9 (÷) 3 (+) 7 (−) 5 = **5**

6 (×) 8 (−) 9 (+) 3 = **42**

12 (÷) 4 (−) 2 (+) 6 = **7**

7 (×) 9 (+) 5 (−) 8 = **60**

8 (÷) 2 (×) 9 (−) 1 = **35**

Page 22: Moving to X

4D	1R	4D	2L	4L
24	13	14	12	23
1D	1R	2D	3D	2D
1	17	18	5	8
2R	3R	1R	1U	2U
2	21	3	4	22
3R	1U	1L	3U	4L
10	20	19	11	9
X	3U	1L	1R	3U
25	16	15	6	7

Page 23: Symbols

✿	◈	◎	✳	▣
6	**5**	1	2	7

Page 24: Multiples madness

	6	3	8	4
7	6	1	3	5
9	3	8	7	2
2	9	5	1	4
5	1	2	6	7